The Hu

Super Dave's Guide to Harnessing Your Greatest Asset in an Age of AI and Digital Expansion

By Super Dave Quinn, CEcD

Founder, Day One Experts

Copyright 2024 KD Quinn Partners, LLC

All rights reserved. No part of this book may be reproduced or transmitted in any form or by any means, electronic or mechanical, including photocopying, recording, or by any information storage and retrieval system without written permission of the publisher, except for the inclusion of brief quotations in a review.

Paperback ISBN: 979-8-9917440-2-7

Special Invitation

Howdy and welcome to "The Human Connection: Super Dave's Guide to Harnessing Your Greatest Asset in an Age of AI and Digital Expansion."

As we journey through the pages of this book, discussing strategies and sharing experiences, I'd like to extend a special invitation. Join our private Facebook group exclusively for economic developers—a community where you can connect with peers, seek advice, and share your challenges and successes.

This group is a supportive space where you can:

- **Find Support and Solidarity**: You're not alone. Here, you can feel heard and seen by others who understand the unique challenges of our field.

- **Crowdsource Solutions**: Encounter a tough challenge? Our community can offer insights and solutions, drawing from a wealth of diverse experiences.

- **Discuss Innovative Ideas**: Share your visionary ideas and receive constructive feedback from knowledgeable colleagues who are as passionate about economic development as you are.

This community is about more than just networking; it's about building a support system that uplifts each member. If you're ready to be part of a group that celebrates and supports each other through the intricacies of economic development, then this is the place for you.

How to Join:

Visit: https://www.facebook.com/groups/EconDevMastermind and click to join.

Start connecting with fellow economic developers from around the globe.

I look forward to welcoming you to our group and discussing everything from service providers to big ideas that can revolutionize our communities.

Together, let's create a space where we can all thrive and make a lasting impact.

See you there,

Super Dave Quinn, CEcD

Table of Contents

Introduction 7

Chapter One: Time is Money 12

Chapter Two: It's Not About You, It's About Them 18

Chapter Three: They're Not Searching for Your Town 28

Chapter Four: Risk Sucks 36

Chapter Five: Can I Just Talk to Someone? 46

Building Bridges for Business Success and Opportunity 52

Do Me A Solid And Review This Book. Pretty Please 60

Gratitude 61

Who is "Super" Dave Quinn, CEcD 63

Introduction

Welcome to "The Human Connection: Super Dave's Guide to Harnessing Your Greatest Asset in an Age of AI and Digital Expansion"

I'm Dave Quinn, CEcD, also known around many circles as Super Dave Quinn, and I've dedicated over two decades of my life to economic development.

I founded Day One Experts and the Texas Economic Development Connection. Over the years, I've had the privilege of traveling across the country, consulting with numerous communities, speaking at various events, and, most importantly, engaging directly with hundreds of business owners through my role as the Texas Economic Development Connection founder.

This book is the culmination of these experiences, distilled into insights and strategies designed to bridge the gap between economic developers and the business owners they serve.

The heart of economic development is understanding. It's about more than numbers, incentives, and presentations—it's about people. Every business owner has a story, fears, dreams, and a vision for their business and their life. My journey has taught me that the most successful economic development strategies are human-centered—those that recognize and respond to the human element at the core of every business decision.

Throughout my career, I have seen firsthand how the landscapes of cities and towns across

Texas and beyond are transformed by the businesses that relocate or expand there and by the visionary individuals behind these businesses. From small towns to sprawling metros, the lessons I've learned have been both diverse and deeply informative.

In this book, I aim to share these lessons with you. Each chapter offers practical advice and real-world examples of how a human-focused approach can lead to greater success in economic development.

From the importance of truly listening and responding authentically to understanding the critical role of empathy in our communications, you will find actionable strategies that can be implemented in your work immediately.

As a certified economic developer, I've had the privilege of speaking with owners of small to medium-sized businesses who are contemplating significant changes. Their decisions are never made lightly, and the insights I've gained from these conversations have been invaluable.

I've learned that while every business owner's journey is unique, certain universal truths always apply. It's these truths that I share here that help you not only understand but also effectively engage and support these entrepreneurs in their endeavors.

Join me as we explore the human side of economic development. Whether you are just starting in the field or are a seasoned professional looking to refine your approach, I hope the strategies and stories shared in this book will inspire you and equip you with the tools you need to make a real impact.

Together, let's build strong thriving communities. Let's attract businesses by cultivating relationships. And let's not just build buildings but build dreams. Welcome to a new way of thinking about economic development through the lens of human connection.

Chapter One: Time is Money

Introduction

Have you ever heard the expression, "Time is Money?" I truly understood that saying once I became a business owner. Now, as I sit and wait for clients to decide on a proposal, I know that while they are thinking, I'm burning cash. Time is, quite literally, money. With each passing day, the chances of me landing the project diminish.

This lesson brings me to my first point: In the fast-paced world of business development, time is not just a metric—it's a currency.

For small and medium-sized business owners looking to relocate or expand, the efficient use of time can be the deciding factor in success or failure. In this chapter, I help you understand the critical role of time in business decisions and provide you, as a fellow economic developer, with practical advice on facilitating swift and effective decision-making processes.

The Value of Time

As a business owner and founder of the Texas Economic Development Connection, I've learned that time is my most valuable asset. This realization is not unique to me. It resonates across the business world. Delays translate directly into lost revenue, missed opportunities, and increased costs. So, when a business owner decides to relocate or expand outside of their current location, the timeline for execution becomes a business owner's top priority. The clock is ticking, and the meter is running. This is your opportunity to stand out.

Real-Life Implications

Consider the scenario from a recent phone conversation where the owner of a growing manufacturing company decides to explore options in Texas to expand operations to meet increasing demand. Each day spent combing through the internet, looking at options, searching for contact information, or trying to understand each option's political and economic landscape is a day not spent meeting the customer's growing demand.

Then, once a decision has been made, the additional cost of time spent in deliberations, waiting for permits, or navigating red tape adds to the stress of the relocation decision. The price here is not just in potential revenue lost but in market opportunity and competitive positioning. He wanted to know how fast I could help him find the best Texas business option.

Streamlining Processes

As economic developers, one of our roles in the expansion and relocation process is to streamline the path from decision to action. Having available sites or buildings and pre-cleared regulatory pathways can significantly reduce the cost of developing new operations.

One practical step is establishing a 'rapid response team' within the community—dedicated personnel who can act swiftly when a business decides to move or expand. Take time to map out all the steps in the process. Now, ask yourself, "How can I eliminate steps? If steps can't be eliminated, how can you offer assistance to make the process more efficient?

This process ensures that all community resources can be leveraged efficiently to meet the business owner's needs. It reassures the business owner that he has chosen the right location to move his business.

Communicating the Importance of Swift Decision-Making

Effective communication with community leaders about the importance of speed involves framing opportunities in terms of windows that close quickly. I often tell leaders, "When business owners are ready for a sandwich, they don't have the luxury of waiting for you to mix the dough and bake the bread." This analogy helps underscore the urgency of being prepared in advance rather than reactive. Be proactive and ensure your community leaders understand their role in fostering a business-friendly environment.

Conclusion

Understand and respect the value of time in the business decision-making process. Doing this will enhance the effectiveness of your economic development efforts and build trust and credibility with business owners. By acting with urgency and preparedness, you can turn potential opportunities into real growth for your community.

Chapter Two: It's Not About You, It's About Them

Introduction

I remember, as a young economic developer, whenever I got in front of a business owner, I would throw up on them. Not literally, of course, but I would vomit all my knowledge about my community onto them. Over time, wise mentors taught me to first listen to the business owner. By listening to them about their wants and desires, I could better respond and show how my community could help solve their problems.

When engaging with business owners about a potential relocation or expansion, it's crucial to remember that the conversation is not about showcasing your community's features in a rapid-fire fashion. Instead, it addresses the business owner's specific needs and pain points. And to know what those are, you must first learn to ask questions and then shut up and listen.

This chapter delves into the art of client-centric conversations, offering strategies to focus effectively on what business owners genuinely care about.

Understanding Business Owners' Needs

The first step in tailoring our conversations is developing active listening skills. That means not just listening with our ears to hear their words but listening to understand the context and listening for their challenges. What obstacles are they facing, and what are their aspirations?

This sort of active listening leads to a deeper understanding, allowing you to frame your community's features and benefits in a response that resonates with their needs.

Client-Centric Approach

Before engaging with a prospective business owner, develop a script. Create a list of detailed questions beyond superficial questions like, "What challenges are you currently facing with your location?" or "What does your ideal expansion look like?" These inquiries help us gather information and show that we are genuinely interested in their success, not just in promoting our agenda. For a list of suggested client-centric questions, visit

www.d1experts.com/thehumanconnection

Empathy and Connection

Empathy is not just a skill but a superpower that transforms how we connect and communicate. It's about stepping into someone else's shoes, seeing things from their perspective, and feeling what they feel. My wife, Kimbra, taught me empathy is crucial, especially when working with business owners making big decisions about their futures.

In economic development, empathy allows you to go beyond the surface of business transactions and connect with business owners on a human level. By genuinely understanding their concerns, challenges, and goals, you position yourself as a facilitator and partner in their success.

Once you understand a business owner's needs and emotions, you can more effectively present your community as the right solution.

Here's how:

- **Tailor Your Communication:** Customize how you present

information to align with what you've learned about the business owner's concerns and objectives.

- **Highlight Relevant Opportunities:** Show how your community's specific features can solve problems or enhance their business's potential.

- **Provide Reassuring Evidence:** Share success stories from similar businesses in your community that have found success, thus providing a relatable and reassuring vision.

Empathy doesn't just help in initial interactions; it's critical to building enduring relationships. You encourage ongoing engagement and foster a sense of community belonging by continuously demonstrating understanding and support.

- **Follow-up:** Regular check-ins to see how they are settling in or if they need further assistance can reinforce the supportive environment you promised.

- **Community Integration:** Help them integrate into the local business community and connect them with resources to facilitate their continued growth.

Empathy is powerful in economic development because it transforms transactional interactions into meaningful partnerships. It's about more than just understanding facts and figures; it's about connecting with the human experience of each business owner. By cultivating empathy, you improve your effectiveness as an economic developer and contribute positively to the lives of business owners and the vibrancy of your community.

Customized Communication

As a kid, I met a fisherman with several fishing poles. Each setup differed depending on the fish he was trying to catch. He could quickly switch between them. Up until then, I had only one poll. Every time I changed what I was fishing for, I had to change my setup. It took time and was a giant pain in the behind. My world changed once I realized I could use multiple rods and reels with different setups.

Communicating with small business owners is the same. Each interaction needs to be customized to reflect the different drivers and motivations of the business owner. For instance, a young tech startup founder might be primarily interested in talent acquisition, innovative ecosystems, and nightlife.

In contrast, a 63-year-old founder of a CNC manufacturing firm might prioritize work ethic, a stable political environment, a family-friendly quality of life, logistics, and transportation infrastructure. Your pitch and presentation of data should align with the varying interests of the business owner.

Real-Life Example: Tell me about your little league

A small manufacturing company was considering relocation because the owner needed to hire more employees, which meant they would be hit with costly employment requirements in their current state. When I asked about their drivers for the decision, thinking she would say talent pool or access to suppliers, she threw me a curve ball.

She said she was looking for a community with an excellent little league. She went on to explain that her son played baseball, and her husband loved to coach him, so wherever she went, she wanted to make sure they had an excellent little league. Little league as a driver was a first, even for me.

In 20+ years of doing economic development work, I had never considered including my community's youth sports infrastructure. Her request not only caught my attention, but as I shared this with my clients for their response, it also demonstrated that we heard her, understood the request, and could solve her specific wants and desires.

Conclusion

The key to effective economic development is realizing that, at its heart, it's a service role. Your success depends on serving business owners who want to make significant changes in their lives and the lives of their employees.

Shifting the focus from selling to serving, from talking to listening, transforms your interactions and significantly increases your success rates. This emphasis on 'listening' ensures your audience feels heard and understood in their interactions; this is when success begins.

Chapter Three: They're Not Searching for Your Town

Introduction

When business owners begin searching for a new location, they often have specific needs or pain points guiding their decisions rather than a particular town or city. This chapter explores lessons and strategies learned from the last five years with the Texas Economic Development Connection, a content marketing platform built to capture the attention of business owners looking at Texas as a possible solution to their expansion or relocation needs.

I have invested much time and money in uncovering these tips and want to share them with my fellow economic developers.

Understanding the Search Process

Have you ever wondered what a business owner might type into the Google search bar when they decide to explore a new home for their business? I have, and it's tough, mainly because I've only ever lived in Texas. I don't know what it's like not to know where to go in Texas. I'm a sixth-generation Texan with a firm grasp of the various regions in Texas.

Most business owners I talked to knew very little about Texas. They only knew what they saw on the news, or maybe it was from a vacation they once took to see a Cowboys game. Their location search usually started with a broad focus: "The best place to move a business is in Texas." Or, in my experience with a spouse, typing in "the best place to live in Texas."

They did not start with a specific town or place. They started at the state or, in some cases, a regional level driven by specific business needs like talent pools, proximity to suppliers or customers, or logistic advantages like proximity to a port or rail. But, understanding this search process is crucial in positioning your community to be found during the search as a solution to their needs.

In other words, they aren't looking for your town. They are looking for a solution. So, your message needs to be about how you solve your targeted market's problem. Not how great your town is.

It's also important to realize that your community will not be the answer for every business owner. This is incredibly freeing. Once you identify your niche or niches in the marketplace and go all in on being the answer to their problems, you can quit wasting time trying to be all things to all people.

Effective Targeting

Initially, our efforts in the Texas Economic Development Connection were misaligned with our desired target audience's needs. In fact, we drove a lot of leads from people looking for an actual moving company. Our keyword strategy worked, but unfortunately, it was for the wrong customer. Our efforts didn't resonate with the business owners searching.

Through trial and error, we have learned targeted keywords and phrases that more appropriately address the pain points of business owners. The more we refined our keywords and focused approach, the more it helped ensure our organization appeared as the solution to our ideal target audience, small—to medium-sized business owners looking for a new business home in Texas.

SEO and Online Presence

Refining our keyword approach also allowed us to improve our search engine optimization (SEO) strategies, which are pivotal to our content marketing efforts. We refined our online content to match business owners' search behaviors better. We emphasized solutions to common pain points, such as how to move a business to Texas, what legal issues are involved in operating in two states, and how to help employees relocate. This method departs from the standard economic development marketing content that promotes the community's general features and benefits.

Engagement Through Relevance

Once you attract business owners to your community's website or materials, the next step is engagement. It's critical to craft your messages to immediately show relevance. For example, if a business owner lands on your page after searching for "best cities for manufacturing logistics," will they find specific data and testimonials about how your community has successfully served similar businesses? If not, then you have some work to do. It's not enough to drive traffic to your website. Business owners do not have the time to explore your site. They want answers, and they want them now.

Case Study: In Search of Engineering Talent

One of the first Gone to Texas Podcast episodes was with an HVAC manufacturing firm starving for engineering talent, though they were in Silicon Valley. During the show, he explained how he could access a pool of engineering talent that led to several patients he had worked on for years after relocating to rural East Texas.

The economic developer highlighted the community's access to engineering talent at a nearby university and showed him how he could build a partnership with the local university. The wise economic developer recognized his story as an opportunity to attract other business owners facing similar issues. Thus, her willingness to sponsor the podcast episode.

Conclusion

Being an excellent place to live and work is just the beginning. No matter how outstanding your community is, its virtues are irrelevant if they remain unnoticed. It's crucial for economic developers not just to promote the general appeal of their town but to communicate specific solutions that address the real-world problems of business owners.

You must craft your message to align with the precise needs of your target audience and ensure this message reaches them at the moment they seek solutions. You can strategically position your community's online presence by developing a deep understanding of the business owners' search habits and decision-making processes.

This way, when business owners turn to Google to solve their challenges, your community stands out as the ideal solution they're searching for."

Chapter Four: Risk Sucks

Introduction

Being a small business owner is hard. It's risky. I thought I understood this as an economic developer. Then, I became an entrepreneur—I got a whole new level of understanding. Until you've felt the stress of making a payroll, I'm not sure you can fully understand the mindset of a business owner.

Add the decision to relocate or expand a business to another state or country and the inherent risk it brings to business ownership, and you begin to understand the mindset of a small business owner going through a site relocation or expansion project.

Making a move involves significant risks. While business owners have a higher propensity for risk, they are still human and seek to limit their risk exposure whenever possible. This is especially true when their choices affect their livelihood and the livelihoods of their employees.

This chapter discusses understanding and addressing these fears, providing strategies to make the transition as smooth and secure as possible.

Understanding Risk from the Business Owner's Perspective

When considering relocation or expansion, business owners face several risks: financial uncertainty, operational disruptions, and the personal stakes of uprooting or significantly altering their business dynamics. These risks make the whole ordeal seem like an episode of Wipeout, where one wrong step means being knocked off course and ending up in the water.

As an economic developer, you can elevate your success rate by recognizing these risks and effectively addressing as many of them as possible. Understand that you are in the de-risking game. Your incentive policies, workforce programs, and everything else you create to help small business owners are opportunities to help the business owner eliminate risks associated with his project.

Building Trust through Transparency

Transparency is critical to overcoming potential worries about relocating or expanding a business. Every place has imperfections, and it's crucial to be open about what business owners can expect during and after their move. Sharing the complete picture—the strengths and the challenges—helps reduce their anxiety and builds trust. They must hear about any downsides directly from you, presented constructively, rather than feeling misled later.

Start conversations by highlighting the positive aspects of your community, but also be straightforward about any difficulties. For example, if there are logistical challenges, discuss them openly and then detail the steps your community is taking to address them. This approach shows that while every place is flawed, your community is proactive and committed to supporting new businesses.

Provide business owners with detailed data about your local economy, success stories from other businesses that have thrived in your area, and candid discussions about any hurdles they might face. This will set realistic expectations and demonstrate your commitment to supporting them through any challenges they might encounter.

By being transparent, you're not just sharing information; you're building a foundation of trust that is essential for long-term success and collaboration.

Offering Support Beyond Incentives

While financial incentives are valuable tools for attracting business investments, they're just the beginning of what we can offer. To truly support business owners and reduce the perceived risks of relocating or expanding, we need to think creatively and humanely about the resources we provide.

Beyond the standard offerings, consider services that cater to the personal and practical aspects of a business owner's life. For example, partnering with local residential real estate agents to offer tailored relocation packages can make a big difference. These packages could include housing options and detailed guides to local services like healthcare providers, schools, and essential shopping centers. Comprehensive support helps business owners and their families feel welcomed and integrated into the community.

Streamlining permit processes is another way to show we're committed to their success. By simplifying these procedures, you can minimize the administrative burdens often accompanying a move, allowing business owners to focus on what they do best: running their business.

Furthermore, ongoing engagement with the local business community can provide new arrivals with immediate networks and support systems. Hosting welcome events, facilitating introductions to key stakeholders, and offering memberships to local business associations can foster a sense of belonging and provide valuable networking opportunities.

By thinking beyond financial incentives, you can demonstrate that your commitment to supporting businesses extends into making their transition as seamless and enriching as possible. This holistic approach attracts business owners and builds lasting partnerships that contribute to your community's economic health and social fabric.

Case Study: A Manufacturing Company's Transition

Consider a manufacturing company worried about the downtime associated with relocating operations. My client community significantly reduced the company's operational downtime by offering a tailored package that included fast-tracked permitting and introductions to local contractors specializing in quick facility setups.

In addition to the business package, we made sure the company connected with local realtors who could help their employees find housing options, as well as introductions to essential services like new doctors, dentists, and even hairdressers.

This proactive approach eased the business owner's immediate concerns and strengthened his trust in our community's commitment to his success.

Risk Assessment Tools

Creating tools that allow business owners to do risk assessments and offer strategies that help quantify and manage the risks associated with relocation can be invaluable. These tools enable business owners to see potential issues, identify related costs, and engage the economic developer on how the community can effectively help navigate them.

A simple example includes a Relocation Budget Template that allows the business owner a framework to organize the costs associated with the move. Create an Excel spreadsheet or Google Sheets that the business owner can download and use to map out the project cost.

Conclusion

Addressing the inherent risks in relocation and expansion is not about eliminating them but managing and mitigating them effectively. As an economic developer, you can build trust and facilitate successful transitions by understanding what keeps business owners up at night and offering solutions that address these fears.

Chapter Five: Can I Just Talk to Someone?

Introduction

In an era where digital communication dominates, the value of personal interaction must be recognized, especially in decisions as significant as business relocation or expansion. This chapter explores the importance of direct communication in economic development and provides strategies to enhance personal engagement with business owners.

The Power of Human Connection

When I talk with business owners on the phone, they often express frustration with automated responses, the inability to find contact information, and the impersonal digital interactions they've experienced.

When considering a move that affects every aspect of their lives, they crave a conversation with an actual human who can offer real solutions. It's not just about getting answers; it's about feeling heard and supported. As mentioned in previous chapters, many risks are involved in moving a business. Owners often worry they might miss something and seek reassurance from human interaction.

Establishing Direct Communication Channels

One of the first steps is to ensure that clear and direct lines of communication are always open between the economic development team and the business owner. I can't tell you the number of economic development websites I visit every week that are impossible to get to a human. There are many places where I can fill out an email form, but business owners want to know who is on the other end of the website.

You are in the business of helping business owners navigate business in your community. Make it easy for them to connect with you. Business owners do not have time to rummage around your site for answers. Yes, this makes it easy for salespeople. And yes, it makes it easy for grandmothers to find you and ask questions they could have simply Googled. So what? Do it anyway. It will pay off in the long run.

I remember these types of calls used to drive my executive assistant crazy. But over time, she began to see the method to my madness and would Google the information the person requested. It paid dividends, as our organization always came up whenever people asked who they could go to for help. People might not have known exactly what we did, but they knew we would help them. My mission was to become the go-to place for help. It started with being easy to find.

Real-Life Example: Personal Touch Makes the Difference

One business owner I interviewed on the Gone to Texas podcast shared how a phone call from the economic developer tipped the scales in his community's favor.

The business owner had not had time to go through the electronic responses when he received a call from the economic developer. That conversation led to a site visit, which led to a relocation. The business owner never did get around to the other electronic responses.

Never underestimate the power of a human connection.

Training for Effective Communication

Training your economic development staff on the importance of picking up the phone and effectively communicating with prospective business owners is crucial. The training should focus on listening skills, empathy, and the ability to personalize interactions based on the business owner's needs and emotional state.

In today's digital-based world, the economic development office that masters human interaction wins.

Feedback and Continuous Improvement

If you aren't tracking your performance, it's tough to get better. Implementing a feedback loop where business owners can provide input on their experience with the economic development team leads to continuous improvement.

This feedback is invaluable for refining communication strategies and ensuring business owners' needs are effectively met. *Kaizen!*

Conclusion

Engaging directly and meaningfully with business owners in economic development can set your community apart. It's about providing answers and building relationships that foster trust and collaboration. By prioritizing direct communication, you can significantly enhance your ability to attract and support businesses in their relocation or expansion efforts.

Building Bridges for Business Success and Opportunity

Summarizing the Journey

Throughout this book, we've explored various facets of engaging with business owners as they consider relocating or expanding their operations. From understanding the critical role of time to the importance of direct communication, each chapter has delved into strategies that not only meet businesses' logistical needs but also connect with them on a human level.

The Essence of Economic Development

Economic development goes beyond the simple act of attracting businesses to a new locale. It's about crafting a fertile environment where businesses survive, thrive, and significantly contribute to the community. At Day One Experts, we understand that this process is multifaceted and demands a nuanced approach tailored to the individual needs of each business owner.

Firstly, we recognize that every business, whether a startup or an established enterprise, encounters distinct challenges. These can range from navigating local regulations and finding suitable real estate to accessing talent and securing financing. Our job is to understand these hurdles from the ground up, ensuring we can offer practical, customized solutions that align with the business's unique circumstances and goals.

Moreover, fostering a thriving business environment involves leveraging local assets and opportunities. This includes tapping into the existing workforce, utilizing available infrastructure, and integrating into the community's cultural and economic fabric. It's about creating synergies between new businesses and the local ecosystem to drive mutual growth and success.

Our role extends beyond merely providing information for businesses looking to relocate, expand, or establish themselves. We act as facilitators, connecting business owners with critical resources, stakeholders, and support networks. This could involve introducing them to local economic development agencies, industry associations, and potential partners or guiding them through incentive programs and funding opportunities.

In essence, our approach to economic development is holistic and proactive. We don't wait for businesses to come to us; we reach out, understand their needs, and work tirelessly to create an environment where they can flourish. Our success is measured not just by the number of businesses we attract but by the long-term growth, sustainability, and integration of these businesses within the community.

To truly grasp the essence of economic development, we need to see beyond the numbers and metrics. It's about people, relationships, and the collective progress of the community. By adopting a collaborative approach, we ensure that businesses are not just passive recipients of our services but active participants in the growth and vibrancy of the local economy. This is how we build resilient, prosperous communities that stand the test of time.

So, let's work together to create a thriving business landscape where challenges are met with innovative solutions, opportunities are seized with confidence, and every business has the support it needs to succeed. This is the essence of economic development at Day One Experts.

Empathy and Adaptability

At the heart of successful economic development lies the ability to empathize with business owners and adapt your strategies accordingly. Whether it's mitigating risks, providing timely information, or simply being available for a conversation, the ability to see things from the business owner's perspective is crucial.

The Power of Storytelling

You've also seen the power of storytelling in economic development. By sharing the successes and challenges of other businesses that have made the journey, you provide more than data; you offer real-world examples of what's possible. These stories inspire prospective business owners seeking a new home to build their business and serve as practical guides for those considering a similar path.

Storytelling makes economic development more accessible, relatable, and inspiring. Use the power of narrative to shine a light on your existing businesses and let that light the path for future business owners.

Engage with the Experts

As we close this book, I encourage all economic developers, business owners, and community leaders to further engage with the principles in these pages. If you're looking for deeper insights, tailored advice, or strategic planning assistance, consider contacting me, Super Dave Quinn, CEcD (SuperDave@d1experts.com), and the team at Day One Experts (www.D1Experts.com).

We specialize in bringing these concepts to life, offering speaking engagements, workshops, and personalized consulting that can transform your economic development efforts.

Join us as we continue to build bridges between business needs and community offerings, turning strategic insights into real-world successes. Let's collaborate to create fertile environments where businesses and communities grow and thrive together. Follow us @D1Experts

Continuous Learning and Engagement

Finally, the field of economic development is ever-evolving, and so should our approaches. Stay engaged with the latest trends, maintain open lines of communication with business leaders, and continuously seek to improve your community and strategies. By doing so, we aid in the growth of small businesses and contribute to the prosperity of our communities and our country.

Do Me A Solid And Review This Book. Pretty Please.

If you have enjoyed reading this book, please take two minutes and leave a review wherever you bought it. I'd be grateful and will go ahead and give you a #FistBump just in case. Also, if you are an avid reader and on Goodreads.com it would be awesome if you dropped a review on there as well.

Gratitude

Thank you for joining me on this journey to better understand and serve those at the heart of economic growth—our small business owners. I am blessed to do what I do every day, and it's only possible because of people like you who trust me with your challenges and ask for help.

As a public servant, I appreciate your service to the common good. It may go unnoticed by your community, but I see you. I want you to know that the work you do matters. Every late night spent preparing a budget, organizing an event, or putting the perfect site visit together is appreciated. Your passion for the community and the people who live and work there is appreciated. You may not know until long after you are gone how your daily work impacted the lives in your town or city. But I want you to know that the work you do every day has a generational impact. The impact of your efforts will ripple throughout time.

You matter. The work you do matters, so thank you for doing the work. #FistBump

Who is "Super" Dave Quinn?

"Super" Dave Quinn, CEcD, is a seasoned Certified Economic Development Professional, author, podcast host, and mindset coach delivering a wide range of consulting, training, and coaching services for economic development agencies, small businesses, and their executives. He is the Founder and Managing Partner for Day One Experts, an on-demand economic development and small business consulting firm.

In 2020, Super Dave founded the Texas Economic Development Connection (#TexasEDConnection) to help business owners of small to medium size businesses connect with community partners across the State of Texas and their economic development teams. He is on a mission to help reduce costs and stress for small business owners who've decided to move or expand into the Lone Star State. Super Dave knows Texas and wants to help others find their new business home in Texas.

Known as a difference maker, Super Dave is an established trust agent in his community and among his peers. He is a highly sought-after motivational speaker and panelist at industry conferences on wellness, leadership, economic development, marketing, and social media topics.

Before leaping into entrepreneurship, Super Dave served as Vice President of Frisco Economic Development Corp. in Frisco, TX. He helped lead a team of highly skilled economic developers in one of the nation's fastest-growing cities. Delivering 58 projects totaling 21 million square feet of potential development, 43,000 potential jobs, and capital investment of over $3 Billion.

From 2011-2014, Super Dave served as the Executive Director of Bastrop Economic Development Corporation. He successfully helped navigate Bastrop's rebuilding following the Labor Fire of 2011, a wildfire that destroyed over 1700 homes and 34,000 acres of the lost pines. Working closely with Opportunity Austin, the regional economic development initiative of the Austin Chamber, Super Dave helped drive financial investment and revitalization in historic Bastrop, Texas. Including the out-of-state expansion of JAMCo, a Georgia-based company that furnishes and installs exterior envelopes for high-rise buildings.

Super Dave's career in economic development began as Executive Director of Levelland Economic Development Corporation in 2004. During his tenure as Levelland EDC's Executive Director, Dave facilitated many economic development projects, including the $64 mil Levelland/Hockley County Ethanol plant, an

$8.6 mil Levelland Industrial Rail Park, and the $15 mil Mallet Event Center and Arena.

Super Dave has served as Chairman of Team Texas, a dynamic statewide economic development marketing association promoting job creation and capital investment in Texas cities for almost four decades. He also served as a Texas Economic Development Council board member and on several organization committees. Super Dave served two terms as chairman of The High Ground of Texas, a regional economic development marketing coalition covering 60+ counties in West Texas. He was one of the High Ground's Education Foundation founding board members and a Top Gun Award winner for his outstanding service to the organization.

Super Dave has been married to Kimbra Quinn for almost 30 years and they have three children Griffin, Presli and Pierson.

Day One Experts

SuperDave@D1Experts.com

www.D1Experts.com

www.SuperDaveQuinn.com

On the socials:

@D1Experts

@DaveQuinn247

@EconomicTexas

Milton Keynes UK
Ingram Content Group UK Ltd.
UKHW040817141124
451205UK00001B/1

9 798991 744027